Stay with Me Awhile

By Loren Kleinman

This publication is a creative work protected in full by all applicable copyright laws, as well as by misappropriation, trade secret, unfair competition, and other applicable laws. No part of this book may be reproduced or transmitted in any manner without written permission from Winter Goose Publishing, except in the case of brief quotations embodied in critical articles or reviews. All rights reserved.

Winter Goose Publishing
45 Lafayette Road #114
North Hampton, NH 03862

www.wintergoosepublishing.com
Contact Information: info@wintergoosepublishing.com

Stay with Me Awhile

COPYRIGHT © 2016 by Loren Kleinman

First Edition, March 2016

Cover by Winter Goose Publishing
Cover Painting by Fred Fleisher
Passersby, 2015, acrylic paint and spray paint on board, 8'h x 10"w
www.fredfleisher.net
Typesetting by Odyssey Books

ISBN: 978-1-941058-35-0

Published in the United States of America

Table of Contents

Nothing but Hope	1
There Were No Secrets	2
I Love the Sound of May	3
Me and Him	4
Saturn Is a Hand Grenade	5
Chocolate and Drama	6
Alone at Her Desk	7
It's Cold Out There	8
The Far, Far Away	9
The Snow Reminds Me to Play	10
Stay with Me Awhile	11
Eating Iced Cherry Blossoms	12
Set the Night on Fire	13
Eggs and Toast	15
Out of Chinatown	16
There Were Too Many Cars	17
I Think About The Last Year As If It Were An Old Friend	18
I Remind a Lot of People About a Lot of People	19
The Woods Are Closer Than You Think	20
Truth Gave Me Flowers	21
Joseph and I Give Her a Name	22
I Step Outside the Walls of the House	23
The City Is Plastic	24
Cup of Joe	25
Tiny Soldiers with No Mouths	26
Before Everything	27
You Have to Enjoy the View	28

Instructions for Finding Love	29
The Wind Is a Woman	31
Solitude Is a Man I Know	32
Neil Says	34
The Body Is a Poem	35
Stigmata Is the Hole Inside	36
Mortality Is Not a Pill You Take	37
15 Miles East of Pittsburgh	39
The Chalk Stays on the Board	40
The Heart, a Lost Child	41
Living the Dream	42
Sarah Picks the Purple Couch	44
The Chair Where I Read Bukowski	45
Half-finished Garden	46
The Lamb and the Wolf	47
I Believe in the Living	48
Her Name Was Pure	49
Living Like Worms	50
The World in My Wine Glass	51
I Let Him	52
Mother's Day	53
Scratch and Sniff	54
52 Walnut Crescent	55
We're Here Briefly	56
Acknowledgments	57
About the Author	58
Notes	59

"Hope is the thing with feathers
That perches in the soul
And sings the tune without the words
And never stops at all."

—Emily Dickinson

"You can cut all the flowers but you cannot keep spring from coming."

—Pablo Neruda

For Kyle, Jr.

Nothing but Hope

There is nothing in the Dead Sea but hope. The rest is silenced by the falling apples. We pick them from the ground and throw them at each other. Quiet now. All clear to move on. I'm falling from the trees. Open your hand and see if I fell unscathed.

Press your finger into the rotted red skin. Bite into the decay if you're brave. See if you like the juice dripping and stinging the cut at the center of your Cupid's bow. Hold the apple in your hand. Squeeze it. If your hand can't smash it, you're only human. Now put it in your pocket.

Walk the street, a body full of apples. Throw one at the clear window of the bodega. Don't try to run. Fall to the sea below the sidewalk. Float on it. I'll catch you by the ears.

There Were No Secrets

Long, long, long ago, the night was a lost woman. The trees were bone, and heads hit pillows between two worlds made of glass and rubber. You got tangled in thorns and vines. Gum never stuck to shoes. If you looked too long at the sky, a hawk dropped you a letter from your future self. Branches were arms; leaves were breasts. Worms drank milk, and fleas burrowed in silence. The world was as small as a pea. It might as well have rolled under the bed.

I Love the Sound of May

A cool wind goes through your shirt. The trees bend their branches in the night. You think of sleeping under that tree and become the branches. Become the leaves that fall to the ground and get buried in dirt and high grass. Your eyes are shelled by sticks and small pebbles at the base of the heavy roots. Your smile wraps around the thick trunk and your legs grow deep into the soil. The night tickles your bark and soft, plump cheeks. When you open your eyes, you're still in the root cradle.

Me and Him

For Joseph

I'm lost in the ventricles of Joseph's heart. But what I would really like is to move through his hippocampus. I want to know what makes him cum. I want to know. I want to hear what happened to him that one night in his mother's arms, but I'm obsessed with the thought of my mouth around his cock. I'm haunted by the sound of his body all torn up and wrapped around me. I'm dying to try him when he's sober and dried of worry. I want to howl from the side of his mouth, from inside his left cheek. But now he asks to feel my insides. He asks me to take off the *do not enter* sign. Joseph slides his face against mine. I let him crawl inside me this time, fill me with sugar and kisses.

Saturn Is a Hand Grenade

For Charles Bukowski

Firepower, she flowers, full of noise, a gust of wind, an orange animal that spins and turns. She's the colored woman at the front of the bus. She's more expensive than paper, or cigars, or new teeth. She's the high rise to the new world, a sheet of lumber dumped into the river. Her horns are smoke. Her books are gold. Her lips suck the red steam from the terrible noise inside her head.

Chocolate and Drama

On the couch, she sits like a blossom, her fingers pollinated by the bees in her story. Books are stacked inside her. They itch at her skin, trying to get out. Out. Out. The light hovers over her like sorrow. Sorrow hides under the bed. She feeds it cheese and wine. It doesn't want to come out. Worlds become pebbles strewn across the floor, ants that crawl and wrap her in a black blanket. She longs to go with the ants back into the typewriter. Ride on their backs like an Indian princess into the whitespace, into the damp ringlet on the book's cover where she once put a tall glass. She wants to push out the walls of her apartment and jump. Return as a sketch, as some character less developed, sweetened by chocolate and drama.

Alone at Her Desk

She squeezes her stomach, holds the skin between her fingers. The fat slides around. She smiles. She huffs, breathes in the sky, the stars inside her lungs. The hour never happens. Time wraps around her neck, smothers her in a black hole. She spins out of control and her hair curls in the vortex. There's no one around to help, no one to reach out to. The earth gets smaller the farther she drifts. The moon and the rings around Saturn become a painting she saw somewhere. And the boy she loved drifts beyond where she can see. She's a deep howl. She's a whisper that echoes beyond the fault lines of the universe, a shade of yellow, a kiss. A moon song, louder than anyone has ever heard.

It's Cold Out There

No. No. I will not go outside and listen to the wolves tear at the moon. It's just that I'm alone. It's just that you make me feel so alone. You know. It's not an achievement to be that pretty, you say. It's a bunch of glock and glick and it's cold out there. Look at my thighs. Look at the scratches and stretch marks. Look at the skin pulled back from my fingers. And you lick the marks; you eat them out with a fork and knife. I've already forgotten what it's like to be loved; what it's like to be. Let's sit down in front of the TV and nibble at our skin. Let's sit here and stare into the deepness of our eyes, then we'll go outside and eat the cheese from the mice's paws.

The Far, Far Away

My head rolls down my shoulders like a cat. It hisses and crawls. My head laughs at me from the depths of my stomach. It's heavy, like a brick. My head runs off into a field of grass, burnt up from the sun and lonely. It's a lost head on top of an ant hill, worried without the rest of my body. My shoulders are light and my arms pour milk and make eggs. My chest is laughing at my ankles. My ankles are sad because they will never be close to the heart. The head is gone, hiding under a chicken in a barn. It rolls over gravel and stones. It's in the clouds now. It's asleep in a tree and dreams of the body tapping its chin.

The Snow Reminds Me to Play

The blouse on my chest is a mouth. The woman next to me is the self I loved years ago. Today, I have no mouth. I have no mouth. I speak with snow. The snow is loud and strong. It makes love to me when no one else wants to. It's the only thing that touches me, that has touched me in so long. Love the snow more than I love myself. Love snow and how it touches that someone else, far, far, deep inside of me.

Stay with Me Awhile

In this sea, we're all a band playing, a band drowning in the things that mattered: houses, walls, the pictures framed with bones. And then, the sky changes color. Wait a minute, baby. Where do you think you're going? Where do you think you matter? Fill your house with phones so you can call me anytime you want. Fill your house with plugs so you can recharge under the whirl of fan, crack of window, and stretch of book page. It only takes a moment. But now it's gone. Build around me. Build around my long hands that reach out to you, reach out for the things that don't matter anymore.

Eating Iced Cherry Blossoms

I get lost in the blossoms on my block. They are pink and wrap my body with their long arms. Pink and soft, they make me sneeze, tickle my nose. I love their fuzzy faces and long fingers, their trunks etched with hearts and arrows. Joseph and I walk beneath them, holding hands and kissing. Across the street, another blossom, and an ice cart with mango, peach, and pineapple scooped in cups. The kids howl and cry, beg their parents for a dollar to taste the cool fruit ice under the blossoms, under the petal rain, pink and dying. Joseph and I watch from our blossom umbrella, blossom home, blossom shelter. Each branch shakes and strides over our shoulders, in our hair, through the street, against the ice vendor's back. When we walk past these trees, these tiny cherry petals, these puffs of pink and tears, I want to press my finger into a cup of cherry ice, into the bark of each tree. Press my tongue into each bud stuck to Joseph's neck.

Set the Night on Fire

My chin tilted toward the sky. I love you. I love you, Joseph. Moan. Breathe. Joseph. Your skin damp and hot. The tongue, a boat with a lost letter at the mast.

My legs are razors that cut the door away to get to the bed. Love me. Love the heart, and the beat, and the veins, and the weak knees. Love me two times, Joseph. Hold me down and bite my stomach.

Joseph.

I held out my mouth to smoke the joint and wrapped my hand around his cock. I tilted my body back and blew out the smoke, wrapping my smile around his fist. Love me, two times. Play me inside, move my ribs out of the way. Go. There.

Lift the blanket. Darkness around his smile.

Knock at the door.

Ignore it. Make the music louder.

Smoke the joint. Drink the wine.

Boy, I love you. Boy. Set my heart on fire. Set my body in the flame. Take my clothes off. Get them off. Try harder. And don't make a mess.

Write me a poem. Let me read it. Let me lick it. Let me. Let me.

Let me.

Eggs and Toast

I wake up next to Joseph. We smile. His unshaven face holds the imprint of the messy sheets. I love the way his hair falls on his forehead, the way his arm folds over my shoulder, his breath—cigarette smoke and wine, sure evidence of our night before we fell into the bed, before we fell into the depths of our mouths and chests. I like to remember this moment, in a white t-shirt and boxers, our legs coiled around each other, smiles reflecting one another. I don't need a mirror with Joseph. He reminds me I'm beautiful, and pushes a strand of hair behind my ear. *You want eggs and toast?* he asks me. Only if you make it, I say. He laughs, kisses my cracked lips, and holds that crooked smile for just a bit longer.

Out of Chinatown

She pushed me beneath the Christmas tree. Almost pushed me down. Ripped my blue grocery bag full of udon, and pad Thai noodles, and dried chili. She almost cracked my Asian soup bowls and spilled spoons. *Go fuck yourself*, I say. She almost made me drop my curry pastes, my masala, my Szechuan pepper corns. She almost ruptured the bag of pressed shiitake. Damn her. Damn her. What did she do? I'm fine, thanks. Thanks for asking. Fucking bollocks. That bag, the bag I so carefully packed and held from Canal to 42nd street. To see this tree. To see this big lit up dying tree. All for her to break the bag. For what? For a drink. For a guy. Because she ruined her pants. Because. Because. All these possibilities. Fuck her. Fuck her for being twenty-two. For denting my rice balls and splintering my good luck kitty chop sticks. For crushing my pea shoots.

There Were Too Many Cars

The street pounded with lights and Joseph was stuck in a subway somewhere. I closed my eyes, imagined what it would be like to meet, to see each other in our heads. But transit, it takes too long. My pockets fill with receipts and spare change. I miss him. It's late now, and cabs swoosh by. His text, a splash of puddle, another missed cab, and another missed phone call. The music from a neighboring club pours into the crowded sidewalk. My skinny jeans are tight. My heels hurt, and the smoke from my cigarette makes me feel sexy, fogs me up like panel of glass in a shower. Joe calls me. He says he's hot and he's walking towards me. The heat couldn't be any more than 110 degrees. I see him, his hand around his cell. And I run to him, kiss him hard, hold his face between my hands.

I Think About The Last Year As If It Were An Old Friend

I don't forget it or talk shit about it. I think of its rough face and long fingers. I think of its smile and large arms under a blanket. I write letters to it and remember it as a happy disaster, as the year when I learned how to spackle a wall, survive a life-threatening illness, and stand up for myself. Last year will be missed. It will be a memory, a place, nostalgic. I will want my friend, the last years, to stop by every now and then to help me remember. *This year. This year. This year.* I say it like I know it already. I say it like I remember talking about this year with last year. Like I remember its smell: pork dumplings in Chinatown, my nephew's milky breath, a cracked can of cat food for Doris or Jack Kerouac the Cat, or even Joe's cologne. I think back to these smells and wonder about the new ones. I don't make any plans with this year. I don't put pressure on this year to be better than last year, or worse, or the same. I want this year to be itself. I want it to take me to a rooftop party in Brooklyn, or back to England, or to volunteer at animal shelter, or to pick out pea shoots from a wicker basket. I want this year to remind me of last year when I'm not looking. I will continue to love last year, and the year before that, and the year before that.

I Remind a Lot of People About a Lot of People

Some people tell me I remind them of someone else. The smallest detail can trigger it: a muffled something in their father's voice, a pulled shrubbery, a heart on ice, chains against a concrete building. I'm Sister Ann's cherished poodle, Mr. Benafatti's dead son, and Franz Wright's broken pen, the one he used to write *Walking Across Martha's Vineyard*. Before I was Lisa's ex-boyfriend or Leo's old car stereo, I was my mother's daughter, her womb filled with pages of an old book. Now, I'm that girl in high school, picked on by Catherine Getty, the one that reminded me of a weasel, that girl that pushed me against a locker and spit on my shirt. I didn't even cry. *You remind me of my sister*, the girl next to me said. *Strong*. And then at the reunion, she still looked like a weasel, a weasel with a family. *You look exactly the same*, I said. *You seem great. You remind me of someone, something nice to discover, comforting to know.*

The Woods Are Closer Than You Think

1.

I step further into the dense bramble, the thicket. The sun shakes overhead. I'm a rotted flower in the brush, poison ivy and the broken rubber on shoe. I go deeper in. Words sink into me. Some of them I can recognize, others remain just a feeling, something I can't read just yet. Further, I see a dragon and his fire. Further in, I see a family of birds playing with a deck of cards and a fox sharpening its knife collection. The worms writhe in the mud and the foamflower suds the moss.

2.

Tall buildings and overgrown glass cubicles could never grow here. The woods are grown by a woman named Truth. Life deepens because of her.

3.

The path back home is strewn with stones, lit up through the darkness. They make the darkness shine. Everything depends on them.

Truth Gave Me Flowers

For Charlie Hebdo Attack

She gave me flowers and laid them on my body. She gave me stones and dug a hole for them inside my head. She scooped out my eyes and saved them in a bag. The weeds grow under my skin. The stones separate her from me. The crowds walk. One million, two million, too many toes and cracked nails. The streets are dirty. People will always kill me more. Kill. Kill. Killed. Truth kills. Truth gives me flowers. Truth tears them from the stem. Truth seeps under the flowers. Under fingers. Under dirt.

Joseph and I Give Her a Name

On a Monday night, we name her Tegan Elysium Wade and consider the variations: Teegan or Teagan. There's hope in her name. Faith. Faith. We pray together for her body to meet the spelling, to know the variations. And then she'll see and hear the middle name, a heaven for the little poet. She is already different and perhaps difficult. But we can't be certain. We can't be certain we'll stay together because we've given her name. There's no certainty in names or labels or the parts where we hold close and decide together there's no other name. And we love each other and for certain people that's enough. For certain people there's nothing in a name. For sure, though, we know her name already. We're certain we know.

I Step Outside the Walls of the House

> "Think outside the box, collapse the box, and take a fucking sharp knife to it."
> —Banksy, *Wall and Piece*

Sharp knife in my pocket—little rebel blade against my thigh skins me. Blood on my jeans stains the hem.

I want to be free. It's all I ever wanted.

To run through the weeds naked, eat cake with my hands, scream at the top of a high bridge.

Bah!

My air. My throat. My birds. My wind whipping through my hair, the hair whipping my face, my face whipped, head cocked, eyes closed. Hands open.

The City Is Plastic

I eat my salad slowly, pick out the cheese and croutons with my plastic fork. A utensil now, it will be a piece of cracked litter in the back of a dumpster later. All the plastic on the table—the cups, straws, spoons, lid, tray, table top—it's all trash. And the cucumbers I like best. I imagine growing them in my own garden. No plastic there, just seeds in the ground, a path of gravel around the bends and twists. The spoons remind me of cucumbers, long and heavy with the weight of the water in their spooned head. The plastic keeps me eating, helps me lift and pick at this deep dish of spinach and confections. I sit back and watch all the people, all their plastic. They look like walking spoons. It might be nice to be a spoon. Even nicer to be a cucumber.

Cup of Joe

Cup, talk to me. Coffee in the cup, say hello. Respond to my deep swirl of cream. No sugar, please. Why, you ask, cup? Why you ask, coffee?

You're sweet enough, I say. I'm happy just the way you are. Look at me when I talk to you, cup. Cup, stop tickling my coffee. Coffee, stop antagonizing cup, stop caressing its thick white porcelain belly with your heat. Look at me instead. Touch me instead.

Do you love me? Would you miss me if I left you, cup? On the shelf, next to the broken pepper grinder. Coffee, would you miss how I grind you? Would you miss my hands all over you, ground and whole?

Cup, why do you prefer my hands? Please tell me.

Your answer—steam. Fog on my glasses.

Tiny Soldiers with No Mouths

I step in the shower; the rain on my back warms me. The incense I lit smokes up the unpainted walls, the base coat smeared by steam. My feet wriggle in the water, in the small lake up to my ankles.

I'm alone. Now I know it. I wiggle the whole foot in the puddle; forget about the mess I've made.

My feet steady me in the marsh where water bugs nibble a hangnail.

Toes squiggle, rub, splash, scratch, and hiccup against one another. They look like tiny soldiers drowning in a row, a small family floating with their backs against one another. No hands to reach. No mouths.

Before Everything

They screamed before they hit the mountain, before they hit the person in front of them with their knees. Before they ate the yolk mashed into the bread, or drank the coffee, or burnt the roof of their mouth. Before they pushed the cushion behind their head. Before they laughed at the fat man squeezing himself in the seat across from them. Before they picked at the magazines stuffed in the seat pocket, arranged their music, strapped on their headphones, took off their shoes, wiggled their toes. Before they flipped through the TV guide, before they texted "I love you" or "See you when we land." Before they had anxiety about flying, taking off from work to take this trip, or before they entered the credit numbers in the entry form, before they looked at the destination guides, before they woke up, before they ate the sandwich, or croissant, or laughed, or made love. Before they cracked the snow pea, before, before. Before everything they imagined. Before they crossed the street and looked both ways.

You Have to Enjoy the View

Today, you put down the cell phone. Put away the cell phone. Burn it. Log off. Pull the wire from the wall. Rip it out. Log on to yourself. Log into the long nights on a lawn in front of your house. The summer air buzzes with cicada thighs. Drink the moonlight and rub the dew with your feet. You're not here anymore. Not here where all those gadgets control your life: texts and TV. You're free now. Laugh, loudly. Laugh at nothing. Laugh just because you can laugh. Take a hot shower; lather your skin under the heat after a long day. Stitch your favorite books together; go to sleep in them. Now stretch out on the bed, naked. The heat rolls off you; the cool air chills your knees. Stand up. Look out the window. Fly with the birds. Don't care about anything else, but the birds. Care enough about yourself to keep looking, to keep watch, and enjoy the view. You have to enjoy the view.

Instructions for Finding Love

Believe in the stars. Believe in the universe, its divine plan to shoot down love, drop its carcass on your doorstep, and leave it there, twitching and broken.

Eat a rosebush. Swallow. The thorns will scratch and prick your throat. The throat will bleed. Cough up the blood and spit it at a passing deer. The dear will think it got shot. Cut its ears off. Mail them to the lover of your dreams.

Slit your belly at the side and stuff in a small stick. Press that stick hard into the skin until you bleed out. As you are dying, call your lover. Tell him to come over. If he kisses your bloody mouth that's how you know he loves you.

List everything you hate, like chewing with the mouth open, farting in public, stealing bonds from the bank, having another family with a woman from South America. You will want all of these things, and not settle for less.

Find a role model, one that steals souls from the graveyard. One that tickles you, even when you say STOP. One that shows your life is meek and ill willed. Find a role model so you can hunt and pull the rabbit apart together.

Give everyone the benefit of the doubt, even if you think they might've stabbed their grandmother. You can't be too unsure in these situations. Keep dating them and follow the trail of dried blood.

Above all, build a relationship with yourself. Know that you are the only one that matters. You are the one who should lie about your age, and lick your fingers in public over a hot, buttery lobster dinner. True love is around the corner, buried in a ditch somewhere. Or maybe it's in your head, the best kind.

The Wind Is a Woman

The wind howls. It screeches, then breaks the living room in a thousand pieces. The wind. I feel her in my heart, a stabbing. She has millions of hearts, all laughing in constant agony. One gets impaled on my knife rack. Another one smashes my glass dining table. The china shivers and the cats squish their bodies under the couch. Now she's inside, colder than I can remember. She screams, sounds like a jetliner exploding in the clouds. The pieces she throws at me slice my skin. No help. Just more slicing, until the pain becomes so unbearable it's hard for me to shut the window.

Solitude Is a Man I Know

1.

Solitude is an old man with fake teeth. I suspect he's unkissable. He washes with silk and dines behind roman shades.

I pass him on the street and he walks on, dizzy in the knees, a creature of disease. A creature in the field of girls passing by, saying, "How's it going, Sol?" There's a blast, a smile across his face and he feels alive. Something takes him back to those girls smiling. Not movie stars, just girls with their miraculous smiles.

2.

Solitude is a man alone in a railroad yard. He makes me feel better about myself. He's quiet inside, like me. Like me. He's simple inside. I get what he sees in life. I see that too: lots of earth, bumps on the ground, sideways nails discarded everywhere.

He wants to be the wild animal he's meant to be, but he can't seem to go for the kill. He wants the woman. He wants to eat her, but struggles to open his mouth. He struggles to do the things that once seemed so natural, like making love, or talking.

3.

Solitude is a man named Charles who reads Baudelaire to his girlfriend in the kitchen, his insane girlfriend who hates poems. His girlfriend picks at her thumb. She picks at his stories and poems with a chopstick.

Her face is scraped away by nails. Charles ignores her. He locks himself in the bathroom with his poetry book, and listens to his girlfriend *Pang! Pang! Pang!* against the door.

Neil Says

For Neil deGrasse Tyson

We're made from the stars, the carbon broken and the hydrogen set against the backs of our fingers. We laugh all Milky Way and sunrays. We sleep heartbeat and moon dust. And ribs at the sides of our bodies are the shards of meteorites that cast out from the core of the solar system. The whole world beats a small pulse at the corner of our mouths, at the crook of our necks. This world inside our bodies is tender and whole with the cosmos. There is obsession in its skin and desire in its bright bang. We are one, one with the whole. We're the whole, then just one. And many again, in the space between our fingers, the space between our hearts, in space.

The Body Is a Poem

My skin is a white sheet of paper. Eyes, two buckets of brown dirt. I don't cry anymore over my curves. I feed my body apples, pears, and squash. I feed it squats and walks. I wash the sweat off from my workout in a warm, lavender-scented shower. The shower is the lake from a dream.

Go now. This body doesn't hate itself. There is nothing here to consume but love.

My body sings me to sleep. My body is ground, gravel, twigs, and brambles.

I examine the cracked skin on my feet, the dried patches on the tops of my toes. I see my legs, freckled and chubby, against the cat's back. I pull my messy hair back in a bun and sigh deep and slow. The room is quiet now. No sound, only my heart, gentle and warm, says thank you for loving me again. And my fingers rest on my chest; they can hear the sound of my heart.

I push myself off the bed and look in the tall mirror. All those spots. All those scars and scabs. All these dimples on the thigh. It's all a poem.

Stigmata Is the Hole Inside

> *"Am I inside, am I outside? The inside pierces me with holes in my brain."*—Hélène Cixous

In the garden, I hear the angels speaking near the clay pots and hibiscus. They dig up the potatoes with their wings. Blackened by dirt. One gets caught in a thorn bush. Pricked. The other presses a feather over the small hole. They whisper into each other's ears about the dead and the living. They chuckle at the truck that flattened the Davis girl. Silly flesh wound. They throw wing to wing in praise of the lost father in that Texas mudslide. Troublesome decapitation. One coughs and ashes the cigarette. God is not here today. They don't like to be told what to do. I watch them pricking their feet with the hoe. Stigma. Tomb-cradle. Keep me from looking. Dear God. They are swinging now in my tree swing. The thing about joy. There is none. I watch. They won't let me listen. They want a password. I pass. I pass. It's misfortune they joke about. What must I give to enter? What must I think? My house is full. High above the half-moon, I press my face to the garden fence. The key wrangles against a loose nail. My cheek is pierced. Now I'm bleeding. Let me in. Now, let me in.

Mortality Is Not a Pill You Take

For Christopher Hitchens

1.

The neck, hot and infected and close to the brain, pulsed and ached. I wanted to cut into it myself and rip everything out. One doctor gave me Benadryl. One doctor gave me pain meds. Another doctor, a sleeping pill. I needed sleep. I needed to fall into the white sheet of paper. I needed to get back to work, but work turned into a snail that slugged along the concrete.

2.

That first night, when everyone buzzed around the hospital, I thought about whom I'd give my books to. I thought about who'd miss me the most. I thought who'd take care of Doris. No one. Nothing. Blank. Blank.

3.

The bed, the food, the nurses, all sweet and nice, all saying my neck seemed less swollen. The doctor. The doctor. His pen clicked and dotted the paper. Dr. A told me *we're lucky*, and the whole time I tried to figure out who the "we" could've been.

4.

I touched the angel's grey hands.

I had the honor of kissing death, holding her hand, tall and delicate. She told me go back. Go back—I think you still have time.

15 Miles East of Pittsburgh

For the children of the Franklin Regional High School stabbing

The yellow tape blows in the wind. The trees won't let you pass. Light turns you into a pumpkin, exposes you to the faces of the dead. The children's stabbed backs sprout flowers. Don't go there. Don't try to wrestle the tape down, or reach at it. Avoid striking a match near gasoline, near crying mothers. Let the bones shatter on the floor of the school. The children grip a string and stitch their gashes together. You can hear their breathing, a rustle of a skirt, the glow of the Big Dipper. A gasp. A new moon. A seed. A bean sprout.

The Chalk Stays on the Board

The ink runs on the fingers down to the bone. Behind the dark board, there's the mouth that feeds you the education that teaches you nothing. I wish I could convince you that nothing is ever what it seems. That chalk is a razor blade that cuts you when you're not looking. That ink is acid that grades the lines of the paper a bloody red. I wish I could mask your eyes from the lie. Nothing lasts forever, not the grades on paper, not even the lines that feed you with their skinny fingers. Your skin looks like chalk. Your mind, a graveyard. Your mouth, full of bones.

The Heart, a Lost Child

Don't touch. Don't touch. Leave the cat in the well. Pull the garbage out of her belly. Throw her in. Throw her in the womb where the worm crawls. The milk is a strand of hair. The walk is intestinal. Slowly. We walk slowly to the store. Condoms and cigarettes. We talk. The talking gets us down. You go down on me in the night with my eyes closed. Down in the well. Your heart is a lost child in a field. The night is a hole in my chest. You walk me down to the shore of an overarching vessel. We ride in the night. We walk on water, and the water is gold. The teeth, rotted yellow. Worms, dirt, light, and tears. My chest is a tavern with a light inside. He licks my wrist. I yelp. I pant. I want him inside of me. Forever. And again. My dirty fingers pick at his navel. Now. Come here. Pull the twigs out of my hair. Put me down. Split the peel from the orange. I like it better. Say yes. Say yes. Swim in the crease of my eye. Now. Now.

Living the Dream

1.

The hands are shaped like a heart, a fist with vein that runs through the torso. The hands are shadows against your lover's face, hard bread and beans in an oven, over a campfire, on a computer keyboard.

2.

The clock has horns. Its numbers are red and black and awkward. I hate the clock, it rushes me, and it makes me feel more alone.

One through ten, then back again to remind me nothing's changed. It's the same coffee mug, the same windows in the same building.

3.

The books on my shelf are cracked. They smile at me. Some of them have sharp teeth, crooked smiles, and faded shirts.

What do they want from me? What do they care if I jumped from the window? What do they care if my fingers never touched their spines?

4.

An ear is a word, made up and silly like *gazump*. Ears make me laugh at their bent hills and valleys, their unclean caves.

I saw a bear once pop its head out from behind the cashier's head, from inside her ear. She didn't notice.

5.

I don't want to open my eyes to see the dead bugs, dead children, all dead, walking around, up and down the city streets.

All of the dead, with their shoes and designer bags that won't save them from the monsters in their own head, the bears that run wild inside their skull.

Not even the cab will get me there on time. Wherever *there* is. Wherever I want *it* to be.

Sarah Picks the Purple Couch

She had to have it. This couch, fluffed and wide, in a deep, rich purple, would stick out in the dark. She'd rest her head on the pillow; take it easy, with a firm hand on her thigh and massaging the soar part of the muscle. The couch would be a far cry from the hospital bed she spent so much time in when she was a girl, twelve years old and fractured by a moving a car. Those long nights turned into weeks where she lay, flayed out in a cast, injected with tubes, taking purple pills with names she couldn't pronounce.

The Chair Where I Read Bukowski

1.

I break the chair and it comes back together. The chair is made of dead women and lost children. It's made from bird carcasses and tax returns. Tape measures refine its gaps and cracks. When I sit, I'm lost in its comforts, smiling helplessly.

I don't want to sit down for one more minute. I won't do it! I won't condemn myself to its cut wood, its nails and wheels, its glue and splintered legs.

2.

When I roll through the dining room, I make the china cabinet quiver. The glasses rattle against the doors. I watch them almost fall and want to throw the chair, free my skin.

Half-finished Garden

The bones of the dead fertilize the earth. I press my face into the cool mud. The water drips from the hose, cleans my wounds. I can hear the worms speaking to me. I'm leaning to close, they say. Then, a bird swoops down and swallows one whole. A worm tail twitches in its beak above the half-finished garden.

The Lamb and the Wolf

For Hélène Cixous

The wolf kisses the side of the lamb, and its head bends like the side of a paper cup. The wolf is hungry, wants the lamb in her belly. Never let lamb go, never let it go.

I want to hold you in my mouth, says the wolf.
I want you to hold me in your mouth, says the lamb.

They stare at each other. It doesn't matter who talks first.

Wolf rubs lamb's head, rubs her snout, cool-wet on the wool.

I want to eat you like a metaphor, says the wolf.
I want you to eat me, says the lamb.

They stare at the moon, at the end of the farm, just the wolf and the lamb. Their teeth, sharp for each other.

I Believe in the Living

I carry James to the graveyard. The wind, gentle in the night. The flowers wither from the stem up. I care too much about his memory, his cancer and his skin drenched in bleach. I care too much about love and the things it makes me do. Morning heads up over the stones and the priest asks if that's all I want to say. I lower him down and under the muck. I leave him. I don't cry. I don't even wear black. The hole in the earth eats away at his skin. The heavy burden of love takes me down and chokes. I'm sorry. The moment they take him away I'll sigh over my cracked knuckles. I'll put my hands in my pockets and perish at the thought of how much I care about him. I'm guilty of worrying about all the whiskey I'll drink. I'm guilty of wishing him dead moments before . . . Take him away. Take him into the churchyard. Take him into the light. All the surgeries, all the medications couldn't save the body, all of those breakable things I call hope. He's a good man. He's a dead man. Think something must change. Think something must get better. Think there is faith. Now I see there's none of that. Because he's gone away. What did I think would happen? What did I think would become of praying? Move on, I say in my own ear. Go on, I say in my own ear. Nothing to see. Nothing to feel. He's buried there. Right there. Under the mess and the mud. Right there, with all that cold running around from above.

Her Name Was Pure

For Kayla Jean Mueller, a 26-year-old American woman held by Islamic State militants

She was innocent, a fresh cut to the earth, a fallen eyelash. Pure. Uncontaminated, unless by death. Unless by dirt and sand. Pure, clean, unscathed, uncut, unsick. The hands blemished her skin. Their hands dug out the eyeballs and fed the lids to goats. The pure lids, clean and holy, fed them love and innocence. Her name was slashed and beheaded. The name. The name felt pure on the blade, sharp and heavy. It felt alone and free. Kayla. Kayla, a song her mother played when she was young. Every note necessary. Kayla. Kayla. No need to whisper it. No need to die.

Living Like Worms

Worm in the dirt, line on paper, pen in the mud, poem in the grass, smile on the sidewalk. Worm slow and cool by the poolside, dried up like leather. No regrets, this worm. No bones, no jaw, no skull to hold me back. Unhinged in the hand and in the fields and the woods. Call me a worm. Call me vermin from a great height. Human against the clouds, thoughtless giant, know-it-all. I'm the most perfect freedom, soil's necessity, pure and obedient, my stomach against the bramble, mouth in the dirt. I'll never let the grass go, the roots tangled down here next to the wild rose.

The World in My Wine Glass

Tall buildings rise above the Zinfandel. I can see people in their rooms, naked and searching for their underwear. The lights on their roofs reflect into the white wine, in the skins of their owners. Once, I saw a dog roll over and rub its back against a red rug. My wine glass is full of stars and sky, a Maine road, blackened by the night. Its shape holds a hill and a mountain at the same time and at every turn there's a man that skis the snowy Alps. I see my mother and my father looking back at me, reaching out with their arms. They laugh because I'm so far away. These other worlds are small stones strewn across a desert landscape, filled with walking spoons and flying fish. Nothing can catch them. No one else but me can watch. I see it all: a broken washing machine, a pile of clothes, and Joseph clipping his toenails on the couch. There's no reason to close my eyes, to look away from the events of the day, peppered with tulips in the grass. The glass is never full, short stemmed, or empty. Many hearts in there. Many Josephs. If I breathe, I could miss something, everything. Like a blast of wind from an open window, a carjacking, or a kiss on my forehead, a hello, a welcome home sign, or even my own face looking up at me from the white liquid inside the lit building, on top of the room, waving.

I Let Him

There once was a boy from Nantucket who loved me under the shade of a peach tree. He kept me cool with his tongue between my hips. He led me into the fields and held my face down against the ground. He screwed me while I lay on my side and kissed the freckles on my shoulders. When I came, he smiled so hard it wrapped around his face and settled at the back of his head. He was young and old. He was null and void. He was built on abstractions and expectations. I wanted him to love me forever. I wanted him to stay to the end and die a little with me under the peach tree, under the dirt, under the roots, to the core of the earth, to the fiery pits of prehistoric volcanoes. Kill me. Kill me. Kill me with your love.

Mother's Day

For Christine

When I woke up, Joe was gone. He's easy to miss and I got out of bed hoping to see him in the kitchen scrambling eggs, dropping the shells in the sink, swearing at the pan for burning the butter or dancing to the Dropkick Murphys while he's slicing bread, a punk breakfast. But the kitchen was empty and there was only a glass of water on the counter smudged by his lips. Where are you? I text him. *I'm with my mother*, he writes back an hour later.

I've never met Christine before, but I think I see her in Joseph—he's wild, drinks bourbon in a paper bag on the bus, writes poetry on the subway.

He tells me every day how much he misses her, how much he wishes he could smell her. So I buy roses, frame her picture, and put the two together. Joe comes home while I'm in the kitchen making brunch: steak, eggs, and croissants with Brie. I slice tomatoes and layer them on the wooden plate. He sees the picture, bends over and breathes in. *She smells good*, I hear him whisper as he opens a new pack of cigarettes. I smile over the parsley and oregano, clean the stems from the sink.

Scratch and Sniff

I loved those markers. I loved how they smelled. The tips rested under my nose and I breathed in cherry or vanilla. Sometimes I'd use both at once, in one hand, and make cherry-vanilla strokes on the page. I wrote to spell it all out: *love, love, love.* I collected vowels and homonyms. I scattered them over dirt. Words looked like glitter. Commas were pelicans, dipping their heads in the salty ocean.

52 Walnut Crescent

I'll miss you, house. I'll miss your heart in my heart. I'll miss your chairs at the center of the large cold room at the center of the cold winter. House, I'll miss you. I'll miss the creak of your floor and grey dust balls from your wide-open mouth. The thought of coming home to you and wanting you when I go. House, I'll miss the sun on my body through the cracked window, through the brown shade. I'll miss your blast of heat and cool of air, the whirl of laundry in the room where I imagined I'd fold the belongings of my lover. House. House. House. I sigh each time I say that word. Like it's a dead mother I miss, or dead child I mourn. My house, sweet and clean, a fresh peach between my teeth.

We're Here Briefly

Joe and I sit on the rooftop on Fred's studio in Carol Gardens. We're drunk as shit, side-by-side, neck to neck, lip to lip. It's beautiful to watch him smile, to think we were brought here to watch each other smile. Our hands fit together, no breaks. I have salt on my hands from the pita chips, and he dangles the tallboy at his side. We breathe, take deep breaths, close our eyes, and sing in our heads. I lean my head on his shoulder and he twirls my hair. I smell Tequila and mango salsa on his breath and smile.

Acknowledgments

The author wishes to acknowledge the editors of the following magazines, anthologies, and journals where these poems originally appeared:

"52 Walnut Crescent" published in *The Moth*.

"Stigmata" published in *The Paterson Literary Review*.

"15 Miles East of Pittsburgh" published in *Columbia Journal*.

"Chocolate and Drama" published in *I Am Not A Silent Poet*.

"Nothing but Hope" published in *The Stony Thursday Anthology*.

"Joseph and I Give Her a Name" published in the *Voices Project*.

I'd also like to give a special thank you and acknowledgement to Claudia Serea, my wonderfully talented editor, poet, and dear friend, who gave her time and advice to shape *Stay with Me Awhile* as well as my previous collections, *Breakable Things* and *The Dark Cave Between My Ribs*.

About the Author

Author photo credit: Gerardo Vitale

Loren Kleinman is a Pushcart Prize nominated poet with four published collections, including *The Dark Cave Between My Ribs*, which was named one of the best poetry books of 2014 by *Entropy Magazine*. Loren's work has appeared in many journals, such as *Adanna*, *Levure littéraire*, and the *Aesthetica Creative Writing Annual*. Her essays have appeared in *Cosmopolitan*, *Good Housekeeping*, and *Seventeen Magazine*, and her interviews can be found in *The Huffington Post*, *IndieReader*, and *USA Today*. Loren is a faculty member at New York Writer's Workshop, and a full-time freelance writer and social media strategist.

Vist her websites: lorenkleinman.com and lorenwrites.com

Notes

"The Woods Are Closer Than You Think": Ending lines adapted from "Further In" by Tomas Tranströmer.

"Truth Gave Me Flowers": For the victims and survivors of the Charlie Hebdo Attack. On the morning of 7 January 2015 two brothers, Saïd and Chérif Kouachi, forced their way into the offices of the French satirical weekly newspaper *Charlie Hebdo* in Paris. Armed with assault rifles and other weapons, they killed 11 people and injured 11 others in the building. (Wikipedia).

"Before Everything": Based on the story of the Germanwings co-pilot who intentionally crashed a passenger plane into the Alps in March 2015. He killed all 150 people on board.

"Neil Says": Neil deGrasse Tyson is an American astrophysicist.

"Stigmata Is the Hole Inside": Based on an essay by Hélène Cixous. Cixous is a professor, French feminist writer, poet, playwright, philosopher, literary critic, and rhetorician.

"Mortality Is Not a Pill You Take": Based on Christopher Hitchens's last book *Mortality*, which he wrote the majority of in the hospital towards the end of his life and battle with cancer. Hitchens was an English author, literary critic, and journalist.

"15 Miles East of Pittsburgh": Dedicated to the children of the Franklin Regional High School stabbing. This poem is based on the April 9, 2014 mass stabbing that took place at Franklin Regional High School in Murrysville, Pennsylvania. Twenty-one people were injured, including the perpetrator.

"Her Name Was Pure": Dedicated to Kayla Jean Mueller, a 26-year-old American woman held by Islamic State militants. Mueller was an international aid worker from Prescott. She had been captured in Syria in August 2013.

www.ingramcontent.com/pod-product-compliance
Lightning Source LLC
Chambersburg PA
CBHW031947070426
42453CB00007BA/496